Spalding's

ATHLETIC LIBRARY

SPALDING'S

Official Polo Guide

PUBLISHED FOR THE ❧ ❧ ❧ ❧
NATIONAL POLO ASSOCIATION

❧ ❧ ❧   EDITED BY CHARLES F. OLIN

SPALDING'S

...Illustrated Catalogue...

OF

SPRING.. **Sports** SUMMER

BASE BALL, LAWN TENNIS
GOLF, ATHLETIC GOODS 🍀
BICYCLE SUNDRIES 🍀 🍀 🍀
UNIFORMS and ACCESSORIES

Handsomely and profusely illustrated, the recognized authority for
standard goods, and the most complete catalogue of its
kind published. Mailed free to any address.

A. G. Spalding & Bros.

NEW YORK CHICAGO

SEASON 1898-'99

NATIONAL POLO ASSOCIATION

OFFICERS

President
JACOB C. MORSE
(Boston Herald)

Vice-President
THOMAS L. REILLEY
(Meriden Journal)

Secretary-Treasurer
C. F. OLIN
(New Britain Record)

BOARD OF ARBITRATION

JACOB C. MORSE
DR. JAMES H. KELLY, New Haven
E. H. KIRBY, Providence Journal

CLUBS

PROVIDENCE	SPRINGFIELD
HARTFORD	NEW HAVEN
BRIDGEPORT	NEW BRITAIN
WATERBURY	MERIDEN

MAINE POLO LEAGUE

OFFICERS

President
W. W. BURNHAM, Portland

Secretary-Treasurer
H. M. BIGELOW, Portland Daily Press

CLUBS

AUGUSTA	BANGOR	BATH
LEWISTON	PORTLAND	ROCKLAND

NATIONAL POLO ASSOCIATION

Staff of Regular Referees

WILLIAM L. LUSH   T. J. LEAHY
WALTER G. TIBBITTS   HUGH J. LEE

Substitute Referees

J. M. O'BRIEN, New Haven
JAMES F. ROGERS, Bridgeport
EDWARD A. LOOMIS, New Britain
W. L. BARNARD, Hartford
GEORGE E. HARRINGTON, Waterbury
————————————, Providence
W. R. TOBIN, Springfield
WILLIAM HURST, JR., Meriden

Club Owners and Managers

BRIDGEPORT—Bridgeport Polo and Amusement Co., Owners; Frank Selee, Manager.

NEW HAVEN—New Haven Polo and Bowling Co. (incorporated), Owners; E. F. Peckham and C. H. Hilton, Managers.

WATERBURY—Eugene L. Jacques, Owner; Alfred G. Doe, Manager.

MERIDEN—A. R. Penney, Thomas L. Reilley, Conrad Miller, Owners; Thomas L. Reilley, Manager.

NEW BRITAIN—W. A. Parsons, Owner and Manager.

HARTFORD—H. H. Jennings, Owner; Thomas B. Cotter, Manager.

SPRINGFIELD—Springfield Polo Association, Owner; J. J. Carroll, Manager.

PROVIDENCE—William J. Murray, Owner and Manager.

ROLLER POLO

✄

PROSPECTIVE AND RETROSPECTIVE.

Within a few weeks of the opening of the roller polo season of 1898-99, the outlook is most favorable. The fact that quite twice as many leagues have been organized than ever before existed at any one time, indicates that many new players will appear upon the professional surface. This fact alone renders the season more than ordinarily interesting. The development of new experts will be a novelty in the great game, particularly in the National Association, where young players are to appear with those who have been upon the floor for years. The growth of the popularity of roller polo is remarkable this season, and indications are not lacking that it will soon outgrow even so hospitable a home as New England and extend its delights until some day when it shall become the great winter sport of America.

New rinks, of substantial and expensive character, have been erected this season in Hartford, New Britain and Bridgeport.

The season of 1897-98 was peculiar. The game was again introduced in Connecticut, its old stronghold, and the season was profitable there, while in Massachusetts and Maine the interest lagged and fell short, because of various circumstances that had naught to do with the actual merits of the game.

✄

THE NATIONAL LEAGUE

The National Association began the season of 1897-98 with five clubs: Fall River, New Bedford, Pawtucket, Providence and Salem. Fall River was strengthened by the return to the team, and in splendid form, of Frank Wodtke, and his labors added greatly to the winning of the championship by his club. Young Russell showed in vastly improved form over the preceding season, especially in accuracy and speed. Another factor in the winning of the pennant was the goal tending of young Cusick, who never played in that position until Mr. Cotter put him there. According to Tom Cotter, anybody can play goal, and he was never distressed about getting a player for that position. Cotter himself played centre, and it was the general verdict that he played a great game, and that his direction of the team was never better.

New Bedford entered the campaign greatly weakened by the loss of "Dump" Williams, which shows most decidedly how the loss of a player can cripple a team. Manager Doe sought in every way to replace him, but in vain. McPeck, Allen, Gifford and Morgan were tried without success. Finally, Dec. 23, Campbell, of the Rockland, Me., team was purchased, and the club did a little better. Jan. 15 the club went under. Roberts and Conway were assigned to the Providence club, replacing Menard and O. F. Smith.

Pawtucket had its usual strong team in Cunningham, Bone, Leydon, Whiting and Lations, Holderness being the substitute. On March 5 Mr. Meiklejohn withdrew his club from the league, accepting an offer from New Haven therefor, on account of dissatisfaction with the decision of the league regarding the playing of goal-tend Heffernan of Salem with the Providence club. At the time of the decision the Fall River club was in the lead by one game.

Providence entered the campaign with a team from which great things were expected, the players being Pierce, Menard, Canavan, "Mul" Smith and Sword. While the club made a good record it was unable to cope successfully with the teams of Pawtucket and Fall River, and this affected the attendance in Providence to some extent. When Roberts and Conway were added to the team on Jan. 17, Providence won 19 out of the 33 games played after that date.

The Salem team slumped badly toward the end of the season, after having made a great showing up to the last of the season. Salem began with a first-class and very fast team, with such men in it as Hipson, Connell, Wiley, Bartlett and Heffernan. This team should have been in the thick of the fight from start to finish. For some time the club was in second place.

Financially the season was far from being a success. Though Fall River had one of the finest teams ever gotten together, the patronage fell off greatly from preceding years. The same conditions were true in Pawtucket and in the other cities of the league.

Pawtucket opened the season in great shape, and proceeded to take the lead and made the pace in brilliant fashion. This club showed the way almost the entire season. With the last of the year Fall River began a great spurt, and on Feb. 11 snatched first place from their speedy rivals by beating them in Fall River 6 goals to 3.

The season was characterized by faster, cleaner and more scientific playing than was ever known in the history of the game.

THE STANDING—1897-'98.

CLUBS.	Fall River.	Pawtucket.	Providence.	Salem.	N. Bedford.	Won.	Per cent.	Goals Won.	Goals Lost.
Fall River....	..	9	13	16	9	47	.627	587	466
Pawtucket	10	..	12	13	8	40	.597	456	375
Providence....	11	9	..	11	8	39	.513	417	455
Salem	6	6	10	..	6	28	.452	433	453
New Bedford..........	1	5	2	4	..	12	.279	183	327
Lost..........	28	29	37	34	31				

THE STANDING—1896-'97.

CLUBS.	Won.	Lost.	Per cent.	Goals Won.	Goals Lost.
Pawtucket.........	54	30	.643	486	350
New Bedford............. ...	54	30	.643	431	400
Providence......	39	44	.470	476	499
Fall River........	38	45	.458	500	564
Salem......................	26	50	.317	372	435

The tie of Pawtucket and New Bedford was played off, New Bedford winning the series and championship. The scores in the games of the series were as follows: New Bedford, 5; Pawtucket, 6; New Bedford, 3; Pawtucket, 2; New Bedford, 1; Pawtucket, 10; New Bedford, 5; Pawtucket, 3; New Bedford, 4; Pawtucket, 3.

THE STANDING—1895-'96.

CLUBS.	Pawtucket.	N. Bedford.	Fall River.	Providence.	Salem.	Won.	Per cent.
Pawtucket...............	..	10	11	13	12	46	.565
New Bedford.............	11	..	10	10	11	42	.532
Fall River.....................	7	10	..	13	10	40	.482
Providence.....................	8	10	9	..	11	38	.457
Salem....	10	7	10	9	..	36	.450
Lost.................	36	37	40	45	44		

THE STANDING—1894-'95.

CLUBS.	Boston.	N. Bedford.	Providence.	Lynn.	Pawtucket.	Salem.	Won.	Per cent.
Boston................	..	9	12	11	10	19	61	.635
New Bedford..................	11	..	9	9	14	14	57	.593
Providence........	7	10	..	10	8	18	53	.546.
Lynn....	9	10	8	..	..	16	52	.541
Pawtucket.................	8	6	13	10	..	14	51	.525
Salem.................	0	4	2	4	5	..	15	.156
Lost......	35	39	44	44	46	81		

THE STANDING—1893-'94.

	Won.	Lost.	Per cent.
Boston......	51	40	.567
Worcester....................	46	45	.506
Lynn..	45	44	.506
Providence....	43	47	.478
New Bedford........................	41	50	.456

INDIVIDUAL WORK—SEASON 1897-'98.

RECORD OF RUSHES.

Hipson................ 685	Leydon.........................	4
Roberts........... 565	Connell... ...	4
Russell...... 559	Allen.....................................	3
Cunningham............. 313	Campbell	3
Bone................................115	O. F. Smith..................	3
Canavan..........................31	Griffin	3
Wiley.................... 12	Cotter......................	3
Menard...........................10	Doe.......................................	2
Bliss...... 9	Lations	1
Everett.................... 5	John Smith.....	1
Conway.................... 5	Staniford.......................	1
Bartlett................... 5	O'Hara.................................	1
Wodtke 4		

RECORD OF GOAL-GETTING.

Russell.........................294	Tierney....	10
Wodtke..................... 232	McPeck.....	10
Roberts................... .. 211	Staniford...........................	10
Hipson..............................200	Bartlett...............	6
Pierce...........................193	Everett............................	4
Bone......... 180	McKay...........................	3
Connell 145	O. F. Smith..........................	2
Menard........................... 117	Morgan....	2
Cotter.... 52	Dawson..............................	2
Wiley......... 49	Cusick	1
Canavan......................... ... 46	Rich...................	1
Leydon......... 43	Bliss	1
Conway......................... 30	McGee..............................	1
Whiting................. 22	O'Hara...	1
Griffin 21	Sword...................... ..	1
Campbell.......................... 16	Dickey..................................	1
Allen............. 11	Heffernan..........................	1

PERCENTAGE OF STOPS BY GOAL—TENDS.

Heffernan..................................85.0 | Cusick..............................82.6
Smith........................... .... 83.5 | Sword..............................82.2
Lations...... ....83.0 |

CHAMPION PLAYERS OF SIX SEASONS.

Season.	Player.	Team.	Department.
1892–93	Menard	Pawtucket	Goal getting
1892–93	Cunningham	Brockton	Rushing
1892–93	Sword	Waltham	Goal-tend
1893–94	Newcomb	Providence	Goal getting
1893–94	Cunningham	New Bedford	Rushing
1893–94	Sword	Boston	Goal-tend
1894–95	Roberts	New Bedford	Goal getting
1894–95	Hipson	Providence	Rushing
1894–95	Smith	New Bedford	Goal-tend
1895–96	Roberts	New Bedford	Goal getting
1895–96	Roberts	New Bedford	Rushing
1895–96	Smith	New Bedford	Goal-tend
1896–97	Russell	Fall River	Goal getting
1896–97	Roberts	New Bedford	Goal getting
1896–97	Hipson	Salem	Rushing
1896–97	J. Smith	New Bedford	Goal-tend
1897–98	Hipson	Salem	Rushing
1897–98	Russell	Fall River	Goal getting
1897–98	Heffernan	Salem	Goal-tend

THE SOUTHERN NEW ENGLAND LEAGUE

The good people of Connecticut received the revival of polo with enthusiasm, after the game had been absent from the State for five or six years. And this, too, when the season opened with the teams made up almost entirely of amateurs. The rinks were crowded everywhere, but in New Haven, where the game was inaugurated in McLay's carriage shop in West Haven. Hartford did not play until Thanksgiving Day, owing to delays in completing a new rink. It was not long before the managers who had maintained the $15 weekly salary limit strengthened, except Meriden. This team was the only one that ended the season with the same men that opened it. The strengthening process continued for a month, resulting in all but the utter disruption of the Maine league, from which most of the strengthening players were drawn. The National League, too, suffered, and long before the season closed it was a common prediction that another season would find all of the best players in Connecticut. The last half of the season the sport was faster than ever before seen in the circuit cities, and more scientific. Outside of the New Britain championship team, which, under the most able handling of W. A. Parsons, an old National League player, had a long lead, the race was a close one, holding the interest to the last.

The following were the principal players on the respective teams of the circuit during the season:

New Britain.—Parsons, Turner, Hadley, Jean, Melone, Berry.

Meriden.—F. Warner, C. Warner, Purcell, Kennedy, Kerwin, Gardner.

Hartford.—Tarrant, Morton, Houghton, Red Smith, Doherty, Cashman, Devlin.

New Haven.—Spencer, W. Dawson, E. Gavitt, Farrell, Williams, Jordan, Tibbitts, F. Gavitt, Mallory.

Waterbury.—Monroe, Griffin, Conley, Williams, Knowlton, Farrell, O'Malley, Shea.

Wallingford.—Tierney, Woods, J. Dawson, O'Hara, Maynard, Janelle, Curley, Starkie, Bottomley.

THE STANDING—1897-'98.

CLUBS.	New Britain.	New Haven.	Waterbury.	Meriden.	Hartford.	Wallingford.	Won.	Per cent.
New Britain	..	8	9	10	8	15	50	.641
New Haven....	8	..	9	8	6	14	45	.592
Waterbury..................	5	6	..	7	10	14	42	.568
Meriden................. ...	7	8	7	..	7	12	41	.532
Hartford....................	8	7	5	7	..	10	37	.529
Wallingford......	0	2	2	4	2	..	10	.133
Lost..................	28	31	32	36	33	65		

THE NATIONAL AGREEMENT

The National Agreement of professional roller polo clubs was consummated at Boston, Oct. 10, 1898, by committees representing the National Polo Association and the Maine Polo League. It is fashioned after the national baseball agreement, and prevents players from jumping their contracts in one league to accept offers in another league. It provides for the establishment of a National Board of Arbitration, consisting of three disinterested gentlemen. This board has final jurisdiction in all disputes arising between the two leagues, and has the power to impose fines or penalties on associations, clubs, club officers, players, managers or referees, or to suspend any such from the privilege of protection of the agreement. Presentation of claims in each case shall be made in writing, together with evidence, to the President of the board. Members of disbanding clubs are to be owned by the association or league of which said club was a member. The secretary of each league is to send notices to the secretary of the board of each contract signed and approved. The secretary of the other league is also to be notified. An informal contract by telegraph or otherwise is valid only for a period of thirty days. Reserve lists of each club must be in the hands of the secretary of the board on or before March 1st in each year. Players named on such reserve lists shall be ineligible to contract with any other club. No club has the right to reserve a player while in arrears of salary to him. No club shall at any time enter into negotiations or contract with any player under contract to or reservation by another club, without the latter's consent. New leagues may apply for and receive membership in this agreement.

MAINE POLO LEAGUE

❧

SEASON 1897-'98.

The Maine Polo League last season comprised at the outset the towns of Portland, Bath, Rockland, Lewiston, Augusta and Gardiner. The patronage of the sport was insufficient in the Capitol City, and on Christmas afternoon the Augusta team disbanded. The Gardiner team having jumped to Hartford, Conn., the members of the Augusta team went to Gardiner. Here, too, support was lacking, and just as the Gardiner management was about to sell the team and franchise to Biddeford, three of the five players jumped to New Britain, Conn. The Gardiner franchise was transferred to Biddeford, but the big strike there prevented a successful reception of polo, and after a few weeks the team dropped out of the circuit. In no city except Portland was the game financially successful. The difficulty was in keeping players from jumping to the Southern New England League, which was offering higher salaries, and in overcoming the expenses incidental to long and necessary journeys between the cities of the circuit. The Maine League was much faster than the Southern New England League at the opening of the season, and slower as the season progressed. The last two days of the schedule the games were not played. The following players played on the teams named:

Portland.—Whipple, Curtis, McKay, Campbell, Turnbull, Allen.
Bath.—J. Mooney, McGilvray, E. Mooney, Murtaugh, Burgess, Phelan.
Rockland.—Lincoln, McGown, Thomas Murphy, Perry, Gendreau, John Smith.
Lewiston—Tarrant, Furbush, Walton, Fitzgerald, White, Gay, Jason.
Augusta.—Dawson, Scofield, Turner, Tobin, Hadley, Malone, Hackett, James Murphy.
Gardiner.—Houghton, Hadley, "Red" Smith, Doherty, Cashman.

CHARLES F. OLIN,
Secretary-Treasurer National Polo Association.

CONSTITUTION

❧

NAME.

ARTICLE I. This organization shall be known as the National Polo Association.

OBJECTS.

ART. 2. The objects of this association are:

(a) To perpetuate the game of Roller Polo, and to surround it with such safeguards as to secure absolute confidence on the part of the public in its integrity and methods.

(b) To protect and promote the mutual interests of professional Roller Polo clubs and players; and

(c) To establish and regulate the Roller Polo championship of this association.

MEMBERSHIP.

ART. 3. This association shall consist of eight clubs, located in the following cities: Hartford, Meriden, New Haven, Bridgeport, Waterbury, New Britain, Springfield and Providence, and such other clubs as may be elected from time to time, but in no event shall there be more than one club in any one city.

The annual meeting shall be held on the first Friday in September of each year, unless otherwise ordered.

ORGANIZATION.

ART. 4. Any club shall have the right to ask the association for permission to dispose of its rights and franchises as a member of this association to other parties in the same or in some other city. In the event of this association consenting to the acceptance of such change, such club shall be admitted to membership, provided it shall assume, together with the rights and franchises of said retiring club, all the liabilities, responsibilities and obligations entered into by said retiring club as a member of this association. Provided, however, that the retiring club shall not be relieved or released from any contracts, responsibilities or obligations entered into by it with this association until all of said contracts, responsibilities and obligations have been fully paid by the club accepting its membership, rights and franchises. Such transfers can only be had by unanimous vote of the clubs of the association. On the disbandment, resignation or expulsion of any club, such club shall forfeit all right to or interest in any funds or property of the association, but such club shall remain subject to all existing obligations.

ART. 5. No club shall be admitted unless it shall first have delivered to the Secretary of this organization a written application for membership, accompanied by documents showing that such club bears the name of the city in which it is located. Such application must be signed by the party controlling the club, and e accompanied by a fee of one hundred dollars ($100).

ART. 6. The voting upon an application for membership shall be by ballot and a unanimous vote shall be necessary for election.

ART. 7. In case of a vacancy in the clubs of the association the Secretary shall request a vote by mail or telegraph should there by any applications for membership, and in case of election such membership shall continue only to the next annual meeting, unless otherwise ordered; but such club shall be subject to all the rules and requirements of this association. A unanimous vote will be necessary for election.

ART. 8. The membership of any club of this association may be terminated:

(a) By resignation duly accepted by a three-fourths vote of all the clubs.

(b) By failure to present its men at the time and place agreed upon to play any championship game, unavoidable accidents in traveling, or act of God alone preventing.

(c) Disbandment of its organization or team during the championship season.

(d) Failing or refusing to fulfil its contract obligations, or to pay dues, assessments or fines.

(e) Failing or refusing to comply with any lawful requirement of the President, Secretary, or Board of Arbitration.

(f) Wilfully violating any provision of this Constitution, of the legislation or playing rules made in pursuance therefor.

(g) By a unanimous vote of the remaining clubs that for business reasons such membership is no longer desirable.

ART. 9. (a) To carry into effect the provisions of Article 8, the facts covered in any section must be reported to the Secretary of the association, who shall at once notify by mail or telegraph the party charged with the specified default or offence, inquiring whether any dispute exists as to the facts alleged. In case the facts are disputed the Board of Arbitration shall, after due notice, try the case under such regulations as they may prescribe, and their finding shall be final and conclusive on all parties, except in case of expulsion, when such finding shall be forwarded to each club, which shall transmit to the Secretary written ballots "for expulsion" or "against expulsion," and if the vote "for expulsion" is unanimous, the Secretary shall notify all clubs of the forfeiture of membership of the party charged.

(b) Upon conviction of any of the offences prescribed as causes for expulsion in Article 8, the Board of Arbitration may impose such a fine as is in their judgment commensurate with the offence.

ART. 10. Each club shall pay to the Treasurer such sums of money as the association shall determine for the legitimate expenses of the association.

ART. 11. The officers of the association shall consist of a President, Vice-President, Secretary and Treasurer and a Board of Directors and a Board of Arbitration; the Board of Directors to consist of one representative from each club, and the Board of Arbitration shall consist of the President and two members at large.

Should the office of the President or Secretary become vacant by death, resignation or removal, the association shall within one week elect a successor. Under no circumstances shall anyone be eligible to the Presidency or Secretaryship who is in any way financially interested in any club of the association. In all cases the election must be by ballot.

ART. 12. The Secretary shall be the Treasurer of the association, and as such shall be the custodian of its funds, receive all dues, fees and assessments, make such payments as ordered by the association and render annually a report of his accounts. He shall have the custody and care of the official records and papers of the association, keep a true account of all meetings, issue all official notices and attend to the necessary correspondence. He shall be entitled to such books, stationery, blanks and material as the actual duties of his office may require. He shall furnish a bond of $500, the same to be filed with the President of the association.

ART. 13. The President and Secretary shall receive such salary as the Board, by vote, shall determine, and shall be reimbursed for all traveling expenses actually incurred by them in the service of the association.

ART. 14. No player can participate in more than five championship games until he has affixed his signature to the regular association contract, and said contract has been approved by the Secretary, or unless satisfactory evidence has been given that a contract has been tendered.

No manager belonging to this association of Polo Clubs is

allowed to engage any player connected with any other club in said association, without such player has been granted a written release from the manager of the rink with which he has been connected.

When any change is made in the personnel of any club the manager signing or releasing a player shall at once inform the Secretary of said change, and in case of transfer the player shall not be allowed to play until his contract has been in the Secretary's hands twenty-four hours, time to date from mailing, as per post-mark.

No club shall be allowed to loan a player to another club on penalty of the forfeiture of his services, and all games in which such player may participate shall be declared null and void.

ART. 15. (a) On or before the first of May of each year each manager shall forward to the Secretary a list of players, not to exceed eight men, which shall be called his reserve list.

(b) Immediately upon the receipt of the above lists the Secretary shall forward copies of the same to the various clubs of the association.

(c) No manager or his agent shall negotiate with any player upon either of the above lists under penalty of a fine or expulsion.

ART. 16. No player under contract with, or reservation to, any club of this association shall, without its consent, enter into negotiations with any club or other association or league for future services, but if such consent be obtained a player may negotiate for his release and offer a money consideration therefor, which may be accepted by the club.

ART. 17. In event of the disbanding of a club from this association or its withdrawal from the association or the loss of membership, the players shall become the property of the association and shall be disposed of as the association shall determine.

ART. 18. No manager or player who has been suspended or expelled from this association shall at any time thereafter be allowed to serve any club in this association in any capacity unless the term of suspension has expired, or upon appeal to this association his disability has been set aside.

ART. 19. No game of roller polo shall be played between a club of this association and any other club that has been expelled from membership. No game shall be played between a club of this association and any other club employing or presenting in its team a player expelled, under suspension or otherwise ineligible. A violation of this article shall forfeit the game in favor of the non-offending club and subject it to such fine as the association may impose.

ART. 20. Any person who shall be proven guilty of offering, agreeing or conspiring to cause any game of roller polo to result otherwise than on its merits, under the rules of the game, or who, while acting as referee, shall violate any provision of this Constitution or of the playing rules adopted, may be forever disqualified by the President from acting as referee, manager, player or in any other capacity in any game of roller polo participated in by a club of this association.

ART. 21. A staff of referees shall be selected by the Secretary before the opening of the regular season. They shall be paid such salaries and allowed such expenses as the association shall direct. They shall be under the sole control and direction of the Secretary, from whom they shall receive their assignments to duty, and all instructions regarding the interpretation of the playing rules, and the Secretary shall prescribe a proper uniform for them, which they shall wear while officiating as umpires. In the event of the failure of a referee to officiate at a game to which he has been assigned, it shall be the duty of the Secretary to provide a substitute.

The Secretary shall also appoint a staff of substitute referees, consisting of one man in each city of the association, they to serve in the absence of the regularly assigned referee, and to receive the regular compensation.

(a) It shall be the duty of each club of this association to accept as referee for any championship game such person as has been assigned therefor by the Secretary, and only in the event of the failure of the official referee or a substitute to appear shall the duty devolve upon the home club to submit the names of three persons, one of whom shall be selected by the visiting club. If the visiting club fails to designate one of these three persons within five minutes after they have been submitted, the home club shall name the referee from the persons submitted.

(b) Any referee shall be subject to removal by the Secretary at any time, and in the event of his resignation, removal or expulsion the Secretary shall appoint his successor.

(c) Any referee who shall, in the opinion of the Secretary, be guilty of ungentlemanly conduct on or off the playing surface, or of selling or offering to sell a game, shall thereupon be removed and placed under the same ban as expelled players.

(d) All referees shall be required to secure from the official scorers at the close of games at which they officiate, the score of the games in full, signed by the official scorer and referee, and forward the same by mail to the Secretary immediately. Failure to comply with this law may be punishable by a fine of $5, which may be collected by the Secretary in the manner he deems best.

ART. 22. The Board of Arbitration shall be the sole tribunal to determine disputes between clubs. Each case shall be submitted and determined according to the finding of said committee. Its finding shall be final, and under no circumstances shall it be reconsidered, reopened or inquired into either by the association or any subsequent committee.

ART. 23. The Board of Arbitration shall at once consider any complaint preferred by a club against a manager or player of another club (prior to the expiration of the championship season) for conduct in violation of any provision of this constitution or prejudicial to the good repute of the game of roller polo, and shall have the power to fine, suspend or expel such manager. Provided, that such complaint shall be preferred in writing, giving such particulars as may enable the board to ascertain all the facts and be transmitted to the Secretary, by whom it shall be at once referred to the committee.

ART. 24. In case a player shall during the season prefer a complaint, in writing, to the Secretary, alleging that his club is in arrears for salary for more than fifteen days, the Secretary shall at once transmit to such club a copy of such complaint and require an answer thereto. On receipt of such answer, or if one week shall have elapsed without the receipt of an answer, the Secretary shall refer the case to the Board of Arbitration through its chairman; and should the board find its player's complaint sustained, it shall require the club, under penalty of forfeiture of membership, to pay the player forthwith the full amount due him. Provided, that should the player refuse to serve the club, pending action by the board on his complaint, he will thereby forfeit the benefits of any award, and in such case the board shall revoke the award.

ART. 25. The Board of Arbitration shall be the tribunal to hear an appeal made by any person who has been suspended, expelled or disciplined by a club. Such person shall, within thirty days after the date of expulsion, file with the Secretary a written statement of his case, accompanied by a request that an appeal be allowed. The Secretary shall notify every club of this request, accompanying such notice with a copy of the appeal, and at the next annual meeting the club, by its duly authorized representative, and the appellant in person, by attorney, or by written statement, shall appear before the Board of Arbitration with their testimony. The board shall impartially hear the matter and render their decision, which shall be final and forever binding on both club and player.

ART. 26. Any expense of trial or arbitration or complaint shall be borne by the party adjudged to be at fault.

ART. 27. The championship season shall extend from the second Monday in November and continue until such date as the Schedule Committee may determine.

Every game played by and between members of this association during the championship season must be a championship game.

ART. 28. Each club shall have half of the championship series played in its own rink. This shall be only altered in case of unanimous consent of the other clubs.

If less than six men of a visiting team appear to play, the management of said team shall pay to the management of the opposing team the sum of $5 for each man absent.

ART. 29. A club shall be entitled to forfeited games, to count in its series by a score of three goals to none, in case the referee in any game awards it to a club on account of violation by the opposing club of any provisions of this Constitution, or any playing rule, and in the event of such forfeiture being caused by withdrawal of the players during the progress of the game or by a failure to report with its team at the time advertised for the game to begin, or for a refusal to continue the game, the forfeiting club shall incur a penalty of $100 and the manager or captain $50, which shall be payable to the Secretary within ten days, said sums to be divided between the association and the club not at fault.

ART. 30. The club winning the largest percentage of games shall be declared the winner of the pennant of this association. In the event of two or more clubs having attained the same percentage, the Board of Directors shall at once arrange for a series of five games between such clubs; two of the games to be played on the home surface and the other as the board shall determine.

ART. 31. At the close of the season the Secretary shall prepare a tabular statement of the games won and lost during the season, and submit the same to the Board of Directors, who shall make the award of the championship in writing and report the same to the association at its annual meeting.

ART. 32. (1) At all meetings each club shall be entitled to two representatives, but no club shall have more than one vote.

(2) No representative can have voice in the meetings unless he is a bona-fide stockholder in the club he represents, unless authorized by the club.

(3) Special meetings may be called by the President whenever he may deem it necessary or when requested by a majority of the members of the association.

(4) Representatives of the majority of the clubs shall constitute a quorum.

ORDER OF BUSINESS.

ART. 33. The following shall be the order of business unless suspended by a three-fourths vote of the club members:

1. Reading Minutes of last meeting.
2. Report of Committees.
3. Election of new members.
4. Amendment of Constitution.
5. Amendment of Playing Rules.
6. Election of Officers.
7. Miscellaneous business.
8. Adjournment.

AMENDMENTS.

ART. 34. The constitution of this association may be altered or amended by a *three-fourths vote of the association at any annual meeting*, or by a unanimous vote at any other time.

PLAYING RULES

1. Each team shall consist of five players, to be designated as follows: One goal-tend, one half-back, one centre, two rushers.

2. The ball shall be the regulation rubber-covered polo ball, which shall be furnished by the manager of the home club, and become the property of the winning club.

3. The sticks shall not exceed four feet in length, one inch and one-eighth in diameter, or fifteen ounces in weight. The crook of the stick may be covered with leather, but no metallic substance will be allowed near that end of the stick. A cord or strap shall be attached to the handle to prevent the stick from slipping from the hand, but it shall not extend more than ten inches beyond the end.

4. All games shall be played upon circular running skates, in good order, without any extra appliances; the rolls to be standard size, with a smooth brass face. No skate shall be more than two inches shorter than the ordinary boot or shoe of the player, and said boot or shoe shall have no foreign substance attached to it. The spindle must not project more than one-quarter of an inch from the skate.

The skates must be securely fastened to the feet, and no player can call time to readjust his skate.

For each championship game two balls shall be furnished by the home club to the referee for use. If the ball in play is batted out of the playing surface, and is not returned within 30 seconds, the other ball shall be put in play by the referee. As often as one of the two in use is lost, another must be substituted, so that the referee shall at all times, after the game begins, have two for use.

The last ball in play shall become the property of the winning club. Each ball used in championship games shall be examined by the Secretary of this association, enclosed in a paper box and sealed with his seal, which seal shall not be broken except by the referee in the presence of the two contesting teams after play has been called.

Should the ball become out of shape, cut or ripped, so as to expose the yarn, or in any way so injured as to be, in the opinion of the referee, unfit for use, the referee, on being appealed to by either captain, shall at once put the alternate ball into use and call for a new one.

In case a skate is broken, and a player thereby is obliged to leave the surface, his place must be taken by a substitute in uniform, but the player retiring cannot resume his position until a goal has been made or the time limit expired.

5. The goal shall be three feet high and four and one-half feet long. The surface must be pumiced and swept before each game.

6. In playing a game, the front of the cage or goal must not be less than ten feet from the end, and equi-distant from the sides of the playing surface of the rink.

7. No player, except the goal-tend, shall be allowed within a semicircle plainly indicated in front of the goal, the radius of which must be three feet from the centre of the goal line. It is understood that if the goal-tend leaves his position, whoever for the time being takes his place, is the goal-tend.

8. To start the game, the ball shall be placed at the middle of a straight line drawn through the centre of each goal, and at the whistle of the referee, shall be charged upon by a player from each team.

A goal is won by the passage of the ball into the cage or net from the front, where it must remain until removed by the referee.

9. The positions of the teams shall be reversed after each goal.

10. Three innings of fifteen minutes each of actual playing time shall constitute a game, except as provided for hereinafter, and the club winning the most goals in that time shall be the winner of the game.

In computing the time, all waits between goals and during the progress of the game on calls of time shall be deducted from the actual time and only the *playing* time of the goal, reckoned.

The final goal shall be the one which ends at the expiration of the third fifteen minutes of actual playing time, unless the clubs are tied, in which case the deciding goal shall be played.

In case a game is interrupted by unavoidable accident or other unforseen cause, and cannot be continued, the game shall be awarded to the club leading at the time of the interruptions, providing two periods have been played.

11. There shall be a corps of official referees and timekeepers and scorers appointed by the Secretary; said timekeepers and scorers to be appointed on recommendation of the local managers, and time must be kept by a stop watch or a stop clock; the expenses of these officials shall be paid by the manager of the rink in which the game is played. If either official fails to appear at any game, a substitute shall be appointed by the captain of the visiting club.

12. Any timekeeper may be removed upon the protest of three clubs.

13. Timekeepers and scorers shall receive instructions from the Secretary, and will render themselves liable to removal by neglecting to comply with the same.

14. No person but the players and referee shall be permitted on the surface during a match, unless assistance is to be rendered in case of accident, or unless upon mutual invitation of the captains and referee.

15. The referee shall have charge of the clubs and the surface from the time the game is called till it is finished or postponed. He shall start and call the game, shall settle all disputed points, and shall announce each goal, giving its time, and all fouls and their nature.

The referee is the master of the surface from the beginning of the game to its close, and is entitled to the respect of the spectators. Any person offering any insult or indignity to him shall be ejected from the premises.

He must be invariably addressed by the players as Mr. Referee; and he must compel the players to observe the provisions of the playing rules.

The referee must keep the contesting teams playing constantly from the beginning of the game to its termination, allowing for such delays as are rendered unavoidable by accident.

The referee must call play promptly at the hour designated by the home club, and on the blast of the whistle the contest shall begin. When the whistle is blown for time, no goal can be counted that is made until the signal has been given to renew play.

16. The skates of each club shall be examined by the referee and the manager immediately before and after the players go on the surface. Any player found with illegal skates, rolls or spindles shall be fined not less than five nor more than ten dollars, and his club shall be fined $100, which must be paid within twenty-four hours on penalty of loss of franchise; the money to go to the opposing club. No player shall be allowed to leave the surface without permission of the referee, who shall examine his skates upon his return.

17. There shall be an official scorer connected with each club; who shall prepare a summary of each contest, which shall contain the names of players, date of game, the number and order of rushes, goals won by each team, and a record of fouls; giving names of players making the same, and the time occupied in playing for each goal, which shall be furnished the officiating referee before he leaves the rink, said referee to mail the same to the Secretary at once.

18. If, after the completion of a game and the decision of the referee, either club has cause for dissatisfaction with the rulings of the referee, they may, by submitting a formal complaint within twenty-four hours to the Secretary, signed by the captain or manager of the team, stating their reasons for the complaint, have the matter decided by the association; but no club shall have the right to enter a complaint that does not abide by the decision of the referee, and play the game out under his direction. Any club refusing to complete a game shall be liable to expulsion.

19. If the ball go out of bounds the referee shall blow his whistle to call time and place the ball at the point opposite where it went out, at least four feet from the rail. In re-commencing play, the players who do so must stand in position to knock the ball lengthwise of the surface, with their backs toward the sides.

20. Time shall be called by the referee whenever a foul occurs. Upon the renewal of the game the ball must be placed where the foul occurred.

21. If time is called while a goal is in progress the play shall not cease until the referee's whistle is blown.

22. A goal shall be taken from either side for every third foul committed by it during the progress of a game. After taking cognizance of a third foul and announcing the result the referee shall continue the game from where it left off at the call of foul.

23. It shall be deemed a foul: (a)—if any player stop or strike the ball when any part of his person is touching the surface; (b) —if any player stop, catch or bat the ball with his hands or arms; (c)—if any player, save the goal-tend or one taking his place, kick the ball with his foot or skate; (d)—if the player intentionally violate Rule 7; (e)—if any player hold another player on the surface or against the rail; (f)—if any player run about or strike the ball while one of his skates is off; (g)—if any player stop before or in the immediate vicinity of the goal cage to readjust his skates; (h)—if any player put his stick between the arm and body of another player.

24. If the referee decides that a foul is made in the goal by the goal-tend, or by any player taking his place for the time being, that prevents a goal from being made, it shall give a goal to the other team.

If the goal-tend removes or attempts to remove the ball after it has gone into the goal he shall be fined $5, and the goal allowed to the opposing side.

25. *Any act by any player, that is manifestly intended as an unwarrantable interference by one player with another, may be declared a foul by the referee from his own observation or upon complaint by the captain of the offended side.*

26. If, on account of the absence of, or injury to any player, a substitute is necessary, and no regular member of the team is present, any person may be selected with the approval of the captain of the opposing team, given in the presence of the referee.

27. If a dispute shall arise upon the surface, it shall be settled by the referee and the two captains. The players shall immediately resume their positions on the floor and take no part in the discussion unless called upon by the referee. Any player violating this rule shall be fined by the referee not exceeding $5 for each and every offence.

28. If any club refuses to play a scheduled game, or to abide by the decision of the referee, they shall forfeit the game and be liable to expulsion; and the members leaving the floor shall be liable to expulsion and subject to an individual fine of twenty-five dollars.

29. If from any cause, during the game, play should be suspended, each player shall fall back to his position and remain quietly standing in an upright position, and shall refrain from touching or knocking the ball. Any player violating this rule shall be fined one dollar.

30. Upon the beginning of play the visiting club shall take the goal nearest the entrance to the surface.

31. Any club not answering to the call of the referee on the surface at the advertised time of beginning the game shall be fined ten dollars, said sum to go to the home team.

32. No player shall wear any extra appliances larger than the ordinary size, such as masks, shin-pads, chest-protectors, etc., to impede the progress of the ball. Any player violating this rule shall be ordered from the floor by the referee to make such changes as the referee may desire. The player shall also be liable to a fine of not more than three dollars nor less than one dollar. Any player holding another or in any way using his hands to obstruct his progress shall be fined not more than five dollars for the first nor more than ten dollars for the second offence.

33. Any player throwing his stick at the ball or across the surface shall be fined five dollars, and for a second offence during the same game ten dollars.

Any player deliberately tripping or striking another shall be fined ten dollars, and for a second offence during the same game, twenty dollars, and he shall also be ordered from the surface for the remainder of the game.

Any players engaging in a broil or altercation upon the surface shall be immediately ordered from the surface and fined twenty dollars each, and they may be suspended or expelled in addition to their fines, according to the gravity of their offence.

Any player using profane or obscene language on the floor, or acting in an ungentlemanly manner sufficient to attract the attention of the spectators, shall be fined ten dollars, and he may be suspended or expelled in addition to his fine.

Any act by any player that is manifestly intended to delay or obstruct the game, or is contrary to the spirit of fair and honorable play, shall subject the player to a fine, suspension or expulsion, according to its gravity, by the referee or the Board of Directors.

34. If, at any time or place, any player shall use abusive or insulting language, or offer violence to any referee, the latter may prefer charges against the player; and the Board of Directors shall, upon the proving of such charges, fine the player from ten to twenty-five dollars, or expel him, according to the gravity of the offence.

35. When any player is fined by a referee or by the directors of the association, such fine shall be collected by said referee before leaving the hall, after notifying the offending player and his captain or manager, and in case of his inability to collect such fine, the referee, for the ensuing game, shall collect the same before beginning the contest, and in default thereof, shall award the game to the visiting club.

No referee shall remit a fine once imposed on the penalty of himself incurring the same.

Any fined player shall be considered eligible to play if his fine has been mailed to the Secretary within twenty-four hours after the receiving of the notice of the same from the Secretary or the referee, the burden of proof being upon the manager, and the postmarks being evidence of the receipt and dispatch of letters.

36. Any club playing a player who has unpaid fines shall, upon knowledge of the same coming to the Secretary, be declared by him to have forfeited every such game to the opposing club.

37. From any fine over five dollars imposed by a referee a player can appeal through his manager to the Board of Directors; but the referee shall be upheld unless four managers vote against his decision, the interested manager refraining from voting and the vote being one of record.

38. In case of any disturbance, unnecessary noise or interference with the game or the referee by any one else, the referee shall have the right to suspend the game until quiet is restored, or, if necessary, he may order the offending party or parties expelled from the rink. In case his orders are not complied with, he may stop the game and award the game to the visiting club.

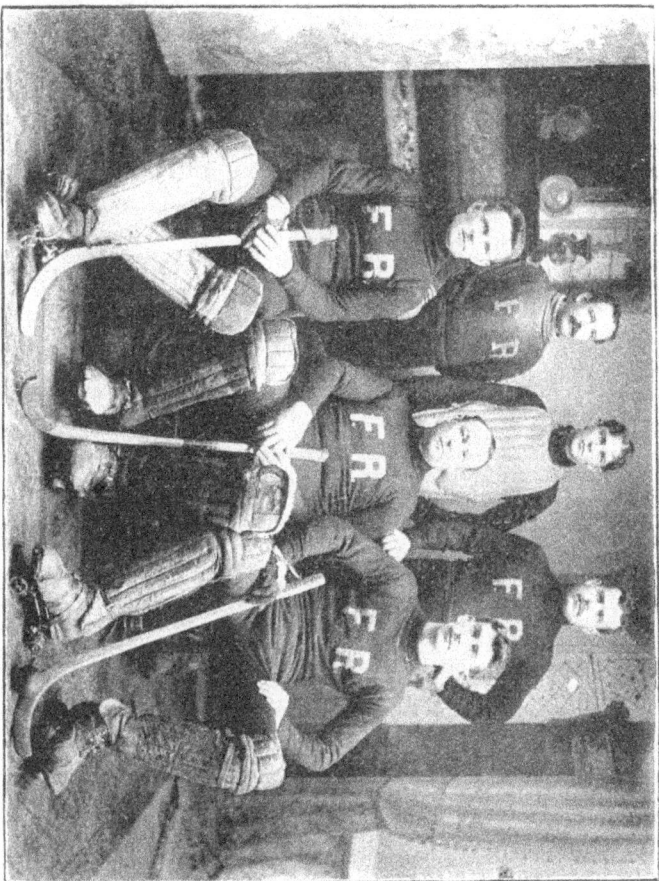

Rich, Substitute.   Cusick, Goal.   Everett, Half Back.
Wodtke, Rush.   Cotter, Centre (Capt.)   Russell, Rush.

FALL RIVER POLO CLUB.

Champions National Roller Polo Association, Season 1897-'98.

THE CHAMPIONS

NATIONAL ROLLER POLO LEAGUE

FALL RIVER CLUB.

THOMAS B. COTTER, Captain and Centre.

"Tom" Cotter is a name known to everybody who has ever seen or heard of roller polo. As manager and captain of the Fall River team last season he added the seventh championship to his record; the six previously won having been landed in Waltham, Boston, Hartford and Fall River. For years he has been known as the king of the polo surface, and to-day, despite his weight (200 pounds) maintains that reputation against all comers. Cotter is in his thirty-first year. He was born in Waltham, Mass., and played his first game of polo there in 1883, with the Crescents. Since that time he has steadily advanced in the game which he loves, until he now stands at the head of the growing line. In 1884-85-86 he was captain and rusher of the champion Waltham team. The next two years he was with the Pawtuckets, going with that club to Hartford in 1889, and playing there in 1890-91, and a part of '92, the Hartfords winning championship honors two years. The latter part of '92 Cotter retired temporarily from professional polo, and played with an amateur Waltham team, because he could not get away from his fascination for the sport. In '93 he captained the club that secured the championship to Waltham. In '94 he brought Boston to the head of the league, and repeated the trick in '95, notwithstanding polo in Boston had proved a losing venture financially. He stayed with his team this year until the pennant was assured and then to save himself somewhat accepted a good offer to play the last three weeks of the season with Providence. He has captained and managed the Fall River team the past three seasons. As a developer of expert polo players he has no equal. His position is centre.

FRANK A. WODTKE, Second Rush.

"The Flying Dutchman," the fans all call him. His position is second rush, and he is the fastest and cleanest of players. He is the best floor worker in polodom, and as hitter for goal has few equals. He was born in New Haven twenty-eight years ago, and first played polo in his native city in an amateur league. In '87 he went to New Jersey and played the three months the league there lasted. Coming home he joined the New Haven team, of the Connecticut League, and soon came to be recognized as the champion rusher. He continued to play in Connecticut for two seasons, going from there to join Cotter's Waltham team. He then went to the Bostons, which were transferred to Fall River, with which team he has remained. He is a superior juggler and a marvelously accurate driver for goal. He is a hard worker, always playing the game for all it is worth until the final gong is rung.

JOHN F. RUSSELL, First Rush.

John F. Russell, Wodtke's rushing partner, was one of the youngest, as well as one of the fastest players in the National League last year. He is in his twenty-third year, and has been playing polo since '94. The Browns, an amateur team in Woburn, Russell's home, were short a man on the rush line one evening, and he was persuaded to play. His work was surprising, and he became a member of the team, sharing championship honors with his associates. The next year he played with the Woburn team of the New England League, McGilvray being his rushing partner. Cotter's team played against Woburn, and the great captain was so thoroughly impressed with Russell's work, and knowing that Parsons was to quit the game, he signed him. Russell was the champion goal getter of the National League last year, and has no equal at cover point.

GEORGE H. EVERETT, Half Back,

Better known, perhaps, as "Mike" Everett, is twenty-six years old, and was born in Waltham. He first played polo with teams in the Waltham watch factory league, and continued to do so until Cotter found him and put him at half back in his Boston team, which was subsequently transferred to Fall River. Everett has developed under Cotter to be the premier half back of the polo surface. His blocking is remarkable, and his scientific passing not only clever but unsurpassed.

DAVID CUSICK, Goal Tend.

David Cusick, Cotter's goal defender, is a "phenom" discovered and brought to the fore by the king. He was the youngest player in the National League last year, then but 19 years old. His native town is Fall River, where he played his first game in the latter part of the season of 1895-96, with the Barnes team of the City League. Two years ago he played with the Sullivan team in the City League. A few days before last season opened Cotter persuaded him to go into the cage until he had a little practice. His work was so good that he was signed for the season, and played every game. He has plenty of nerve, a good eye and excellent judgment, and in one season has won a reputation as one of the best men in front of a polo cage.

RICH, Substitute.

Rich, the substitute of the Fall River team, did some excellent and timely work last season, notably in the important game with Pawtucket, in which he won the game for his team by a pretty drive.

Malone, Half Back.   Hadley, Rush.   C. F. Olin,   Jean, Centre.   Berry, Goal.
                                    (Assistant Manager).
              Parsons, Rush (Capt., Manager).   Turner, Rush.

NEW BRITAIN POLO CLUB.

Champions Southern New England Roller Polo League, Season 1897-'98.

SOUTHERN NEW ENGLAND LEAGUE

⚜

NEW BRITAIN CLUB.

W. A. PARSONS, Proprietor, Manager, Captain, Rush.

William A. Parsons, whose work may be said to have brought the pennant to New Britain, was the fastest player of the league, and the most accurate and terrific drive for goal. He is a gentleman on the surface as well as off it, and in all the time he has been playing he has never committed a foul. He had the respect and affection of his men, and is a second Cotter in the developing of amateurs. None know the scientific points of the game better than he. He was born in Worcester, May 20, 1867, and began playing polo while a skate boy, with the New Britain team, in '84. He played in New Britain the following season, going to Hartford the next year, then to New Haven and to Bridgeport, joining the latter team the last of the season. He played with Bridgeport in '90, when he again went to New Britain. In '91 he played with Hartford, after which he retired from the surface, and for two years was in the employ of the Civil engineering department of the Consolidated Railroad. In '93 he got into the game again, signing with Providence. The following year he was first rush on the Boston championship team, and was with the team when it was transferred to Fall River, where he played the next year. At this time he again quit the game to accept the appointment of street commissioner of the city of New Britain. He has been a member of five championship teams, to wit: Hartford, New Haven, Bridgeport, Boston, New Britain. Mr. Parsons is the owner of the present New Britain club of the National Polo Association, but it is doubtful if he plays this season, except occasionally.

WENDELL H. HADLEY, Rush.

Hadley joined the team early in January, coming from the Gardiner team of the Maine League. He is a clever juggler and a good goal getter. He is now in his twenty-seventh year, and was born in Waltham. He began playing polo in an amateur league in Waltham, in 1890, as a goal tend. In '93 he was a substitute on Cotter's Boston team, and the following season played a good game at centre for Pawtucket. In '95 he played with the Stonehams and Walthams, in the New England League, and in '97 went to Portland, where he played centre. Early last season he was with Augusta of the Maine League, until that club disbanded, when he, with most of his associates, went to Gardiner. Hadley is one of the most genial and popular fellows on the surface.

CHARLES G. TURNER, Rush.

Was born in New London in 1874. His present home is in Westerly, R. I. He is a clean player, working hard and effectively every moment the ball is in play, and was accounted one of the best and fastest rushers of the league. He began playing in amateur games in Westerly in the early part of the current decade, and in '93 was first rush of the Westerly amateur team that played the season through without losing a game. In '96 he went to Augusta, where he at once became popular, both as a player and a gentleman. He came to New Britain from Gardiner about the middle of January. He is very quick on rolls, courageous and wise in the game.

FRED A. JEAN, Center.

Strong and powerfully built, always the same cool-headed, careful player, Jean came to be the king of the league centers. He is a French Canadian by birth, stands six feet high, and weighs 190 pounds. He is an athlete in the fullest sense of the word. He is in his twenty-third year. He began playing polo in amateur teams in Fall River in '95. Early last season he was signed by Portland, but was not successful, and was released by Manager Burnham to come to New Britain. Manager Parsons developed Jean rapidly, and has absolute faith in the future career of his "find" on the polo surface. Jean is the only member of last season's team who will play on the New Britain team this year.

JOHN H. MALONE, Half Back.

Malone joined the team New Year's Day, and his work was enthusiastically received. His blocking and ankle running were ever afterward features of the home games. He was born in New Bedford in '65, and played his first game of polo in the Fall River City Amateur League twenty years later. Tom Cotter signed him two seasons later as substitute, and he did excellent work whenever opportunity offered. He began last season with Augusta, and when that team disbanded for lack of patronage Manager Parsons succeeded in securing him. He was known throughout the circuit as "Happy Jack." Malone plays with Bridgeport this season.

JOHN W. BERRY, Goal Tend.

During the latter end of the season, Berry developed into one of the best men in front of a cage in the league. He is a native of Westerly, R. I., and is in his twenty-sixth year. His weight is 190 pounds. He first played polo on the amateur Westerly team in '93, his team winning the State amateur championship and a gold medal. In '96 he joined the Augusta team of the Maine League. He was the only member of the original New Britain team last season, with the exception of Parsons, who finished the season with the team, every other position having been strengthened.

J. Mooney, Rush.   Murtaugh, Half Back.   F. Mooney, Centre.
McGilvray, Rush.   Phelan, Captain.   Burgess, Goal.

BATH POLO CLUB.

Champions Maine Polo League, Season 1897-'98.

MAINE POLO LEAGUE

•   ✄

BATH POLO TEAM.

J. P. MOONEY, First Rush.

The first rush of the champion Bath team, J. P. Mooney, was born in Salem in 1872. He first played polo with amateur teams in Salem, and developed rapidly into an expert. In '95 he played with the championship Clinton club, of the New England League, having played professionally the year previous with the Waltham club, in the same league. He has also played with the Boston National League team, and with Stoneham club. In '96 he joined the Bath team, and has played there until this season.

N. J. McGILVRAY, Second Rush.

Neil J. McGilvray, as a floor worker, last year had no equal outside the National League. He is regarded as a coming Wodtke by those who have seen his work. He is one of the youngest players on the surface, having just passed his twentieth birthday. Medford, Mass., is his native town, but for the past seventeen years his home has been in Woburn, where he started to play polo as an amateur in '93. The next year he was with the Woburn club of the New England League. In '95 he started in the season with the Fall Rivers of the National League, but was sold to Bath, where he has played every season since. Last season the National League offered the Bath management $500 for his release, as he was wanted to strengthen a weak team, but he was not allowed to go.

EDWARD J. MOONEY, Center.

Mr. Mooney, at center, was king in the Maine League last season. He is a brother of Jimmie the rusher, and was born in Salem. After going through the usual experience as an amateur, he played his first game as a professional with the Waltham team of the New England League in '94. He was with the Stoneham club in '96 until December, when he joined the Bath team.

WALTER A. MURTAUGH, Half Back.

Mr. Murtaugh is beyond all question one of the coming crackajacks of the polo surface. He plays a smooth, easy and scientific game, and is always a gentleman. He is in his twenty-sixth year, and hails from Fall River. He played with amateur teams in his own town, Providence and New Bedford. His career in the game as a professional dates from December, '96, when he engaged with the Bath management, with which he has been since. Mr. Murtaugh has been a bridegroom since the close of last season.

JOHN BURGESS, Goal Tend.

Born in Fall River, twenty-four years ago, Mr. Burgess is to-day one of the best goal defenders in the game. He is one of the many strong players the amateur teams of Fall River have given to the professional polo surface. Since leaving amateur teams, in '97, he has played with Bath.

J. PHELAN, Captain.

Mr. Phelan is an expert, and has wide experience, his polo career starting back in 1882, in Portland. He has played in all the New England States, and in the cities of New York, Brooklyn and in New Jersey. He had retired from the game, when in '96 he was induced by Mr. Donnell, the manager of the Bath team, to assume the captaincy. He has been with the team since, and while seldom appearing on the floor, his faithful work in his position was, nevertheless, a considerable contributor to the pennant winning success of the Bath team.

...SCHEDULE, 1898-'99...

CLUBS.	In Bridgeport.	In Hartford.	In Meriden.	In New Britain.	In New Haven.	In Providence.	In Springfield.	In Waterbury.
Bridgeport	....	Nov. 26, Dec. 17, 31, Feb. 11	Dec. 3, 21, Jan. 7, 28, Mar. 1	Nov. 7, 28, Jan. 2, 30, Feb. 20	Nov. 25, Dec. 23, Jan. 20, 27, Mar. 3	Nov. 19, Dec. 10, Jan. 14, Feb. 6	Nov. 18, Dec. 9, Jan. 13, Feb. 13, 24	Nov. 11, 24, Dec. 2, 16, 26, Jan. 18, Feb. 3
Hartford	Dec. 1, 22, Jan. 5, Feb. 16, 23	....	Nov. 23, Dec. 7, Jan. 11, 18, Feb. 15	Nov. 17, Dec. 12, 29, Jan. 23, Feb. 27	Nov. 9, Dec. 2, 30, Feb. 3, 10	Nov. 14, Dec. 5, Jan. 2, 30, Feb. 18	Nov. 11, 24, Dec. 16, 26, Jan. 16, Feb. 6, 22, Mar. 3	Nov. 25, Dec. 23, Jan. 13, 27, Feb. 24
Meriden	Nov. 17, Dec. 6, 27, Jan. 31, Feb. 21	Nov. 22, Dec. 20, Jan. 3, 10, Feb. 7	....	Nov. 10, 24, Dec. 26, Jan. 16, Feb. 9, Mar. 2	Nov. 29, Dec. 13, Jan. 6, 24, Feb. 14	Nov. 21, Dec. 12, Jan. 9, 23, Feb. 20	Nov. 7, 28, Dec. 19, Feb. 8, 27	Nov. 18, Dec. 9, 30, Jan. 2, 20, Feb. 17
New Britain	Nov. 8, Dec. 13, Jan. 2, 3, 24, Feb. 28	Nov. 19, Dec. 10, Jan. 14, 28, Feb. 25	Nov. 12, 24, Dec. 17, 26, Feb. 1, 18	....	Nov. 18, Dec. 9, Jan. 13, Feb. 17, 24	Nov. 26, Dec. 24, Jan. 21, Feb. 4, Mar. 4	Dec. 2, 30, Jan. 20, Feb. 10	Nov. 30, Dec 21, Jan. 6, Feb. 8
New Haven	Dec. 8, 29, Jan. 12, Feb. 2, Mar. 4	Nov. 8, Dec. 3, 24, Feb. 4, Mar. 4	Nov. 16, Dec. 14, 28, Jan. 21, Feb. 11	Nov. 21, Dec. 19, Jan. 9, Feb. 6	....	Nov. 7, 24, Dec. 17, 26, Jan. 16, Feb. 18	Nov. 14, Dec. 5, Jan. 2, 23, Feb. 20	Nov. 23, Jan. 4, 25, Feb. 15, 22
Providence	Nov. 22, Dec. 15, Jan. 19, Feb. 7	Nov. 15, Dec. 6, Jan. 17, 24, Feb. 14	Nov. 9, 30, Jan. 4, Feb. 8, 22	Dec. 1, 22, Jan. 12, Feb. 2, 23	Nov. 11, 24, Dec. 16, 26, Jan. 31, Feb. 28	....	Nov. 25, Dec. 23, Jan. 6, 27, Feb. 17	Nov. 16, Dec. 7, 28, Feb. 10, Mar. 3
Springfield	Nov. 15, 29, Dec. 20, Jan. 17, Feb. 14	Nov. 12, 24, Dec. 18, 26, Jan. 21, 31, Feb. 21	Nov. 19, Dec. 24, Jan. 14, 25, Mar. 4	Dec. 8, Jan. 5, 26, Feb. 16	Nov. 22, Dec. 6, 27, Jan. 2, 10, Feb. 7	Dec. 3, 31, Jan. 7, Feb. 11, 25	....	Nov. 9, Dec. 14, Jan. 11, Feb. 1, Mar. 1
Waterbury	Nov. 10, 24, Dec. 26, Jan. 10, 26, Feb. 9	Nov. 29, Dec. 27, Jan. 7, Feb. 18, 28	Nov. 26, Dec. 10, 31, Jan. 2, Feb. 4, 28	Nov. 14, Dec. 5, 15, Jan. 19, Feb. 13	Nov. 15, Dec. 20, Jan. 3, 17, Feb. 21	Nov. 12, 28, Dec. 19, Jan. 28, Feb. 27	Nov. 21, Dec. 12, Jan. 9, 30	....

The Spalding League... Polo Ball

HIGHEST QUALITY

Adopted by the leading Associations as the Regulation Polo Ball

No. 1. Spalding's Official Polo Ball, $1.00

I hereby Certify *that the Spalding League Polo Ball is the Official Ball of the National Polo Association, and must be used in all games.*

Secretary

Made of the very best material, according to the latest Polo regulations. None genuine without our trade mark on each ball and box. Each ball wrapped in tin foil and put in a separate box and sealed, in accordance with the latest League regulations.

....Practice Balls....

No. 2. Regulation size, ... Each, 25c.
No. 3. Regulation size, ... Each, 15c.

Our Complete Catalogue of Athletic Goods and Uniforms Sent Free.......

A. G. Spalding & Bros.
NEW YORK AND CHICAGO

Polo Sticks

No. **AA**. "Highest Quality" Polo Stick, made of the finest second growth hickory, and modeled after the latest and most approved pattern,
Each, **75c.**

No. **A**. "League" Polo Stick, fine second growth hickory, handsomely finished,
Each, **50c.**

No. **B**. "Standard" Polo Stick, made of selected material and nicely finished, **25c.**

No. **D**. "Junior" Polo Stick, . . **10c.**

No. **E**. Boys' Polo Stick, . . . **5c.**

Polo Leg and Shin Guards

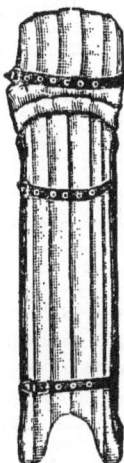

An extremely useful article for protecting the ankles and legs from accidental hits.

Shin Guards

No.		Per pair.
10.	Canvas, . . .	**$1.00**
20.	Moleskin, . .	**1.25**
30.	Leather, . . .	**1.50**

Leg Guards

No. **4.**	Leather, . .	**$2.50**
No. **5.**	Canvas, . .	**2.00**

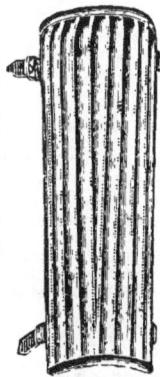

Our Complete Catalogue of Athletic Goods and Uniforms Sent Free.

Front. Rear.

Shin Guard.

A. G. Spalding & Bros.

NEW YORK ...":... CHICAGO

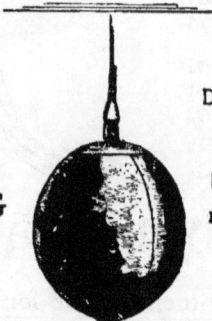

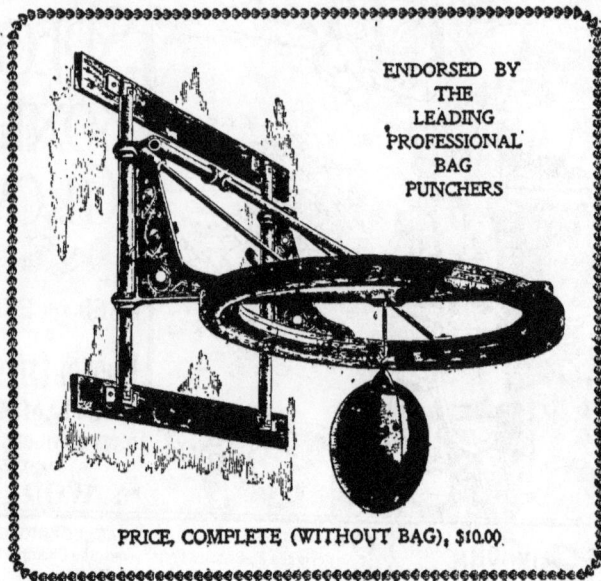

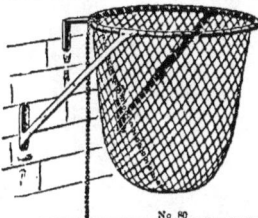

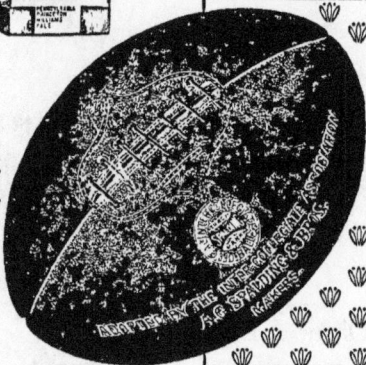

SPALDING'S BASE BALL UNIFORMS

Our line of flannels for Base Ball Uniforms consists of the best qualities in their respective grades and the most desirable colors for Base Ball Uniforms. Each grade is kept up to the highest point of excellence, and quality improved wherever possible every season. Owing to the heavy weight flannels used in our Nos. 0 and 1 Uniforms, we have found it desirable, after many years of experience, to use a little lighter weight material for the shirts; this makes them more comfortable, much cooler, and wear just as well as the heavier weight.

The Spalding UNIFORM No. 0

The workmanship and material of this outfit is of the very highest quality throughout, and special care has been taken to make this uniform superior to anything offered in this line. Used almost exclusively by all League and professional clubs for years past, is sufficient evidence of its quality and durability. Colors: White, Pearl Gray, Yale Gray, Light Gray, Dark Gray, Black, Maroon, Royal Blue, Old Gold, Navy Blue, Brown, Green.

No. 0 The Spalding Shirt, any style,	$5.50
No. 0 The Spalding Padded Pants, any style,	6.00
No. 3/0 The Spalding Stockings,	1.50
No. 0 Quality Cap, any style,	1.00
No. 3/0 Web Belt, leather lined,	.75
	$14.75

University No. 1

In workmanship and quality of material equal to our No. 0 Uniform, but made of little lighter weight flannel. Colors: White, Pearl Gray, Yale Gray, Light Gray, Dark Gray, Black, Maroon, Royal Blue, Old Gold, Navy Blue, Brown, Green.

No. 1 University Shirt, any style,	$4.50
No. 1 University Padded Pants, any style,	4.50
First Quality Cap, any style,	.75
No. 47 Web or all Leather Belts,	.50
No. 1 Stockings,	1.00
	$11.25

Interscholastic No. 2

Made of same grade of material as our higher-priced uniforms, but of lighter weight flannel. Substantially made and a most serviceable outfit. Colors: White, Pearl Gray, Yale Gray, Light Gray, Dark Gray, Black, Maroon, Royal Blue, Old Gold, Navy Blue, Brown, Green.

No. 2 Interscholastic Shirt, any style,	$3.75
No. 2 Interscholastic Pants, padded, any style,	3.50
First Quality Cap, any style,	.75
No. 23 Web Belt,	.25
No. 2 Wool Stockings,	.75
	$9.00

Club Special No. 3

Made of good quality flannel in a variety of very desirable patterns. Well finished and a most excellent outfit for amateur clubs. Colors: White, Pearl Gray, Yale Gray, Light Gray, Dark Gray, Black, Maroon, Royal Blue, Navy Blue, Brown.

No. 3 Club Special Shirt, any style,	$2.50
No. 3 Club Special Pants, padded, any style,	2.50
Third Quality Cap,	.50
No. 23 Web Belt,	.25
No. 3 Stocking,	.50
	$6.25

Amateur Special No. 4

The cheapest outfit we make this season. Made of fair quality flannel and compares favorably with uniforms of other makers quoted at a much higher price. Colors: White, Light Gray, Blue Gray, Brown Mix, Dark Gray.

No. 4 Amateur Special Shirt, any style,	$1.85
No. 4 Amateur Special Pants, padded, any style,	1.75
Fourth Quality Cap,	.40
No. 4 Web Belt,	.25
No. 4 Stockings,	.25
	$4.50

Above prices include lettering on Shirts. Detachable Sleeves, 50c. per shirt extra. Special measurement blanks and samples on application.

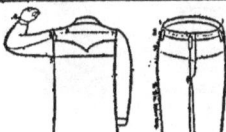

HOW TO ORDER UNIFORMS.—Samples of flannels and special measurement blanks mailed to clubs and others interested on application. If in a hurry for uniforms, and no sample or measurement blanks on hand, follow the instructions given below, give us an idea of color desired and we will use our judgment in getting up same. Our many years of experience will enable us to make a more pleasing combination than parties unused to selecting materials and trimmings for uniforms,

TO MEASURE FOR UNIFORMS.—Cut out bottom line on this page, paste at top of letter, and enter and measure each man separately, as indicated by the numbers given and shown on diagrams. Use this form in absence of special measurement blanks.

DIAGRAMS FOR MEASUREMENTS.

NAMES	SHIRTS				PANTS				Cap Size	Hose	Shoes
	Collar	Sleeve 2 to 4	Chest 5—5	Yoke 7 to 8	Around Waist 1—1	Outseam 2 to 4	Inseam 5 to 6	Around Hips 7—7			

NEW YORK **A. G. SPALDING & BROS.** CHICAGO

SPALDING'S ATHLETIC LIBRARY

PUBLISHED MONTHLY, EACH NUMBER COMPLETE.
PER COPY, 10 CENTS.

No. 70. OFFICIAL FOOT BALL GUIDE

Revised by Walter Camp. New Rules and Referee's Book. Hints to Beginners and How to Develop a Team, by Walter Camp; All-America Teams for 1897; Scores of 1896; Portraits of all Leading Players.

Postpaid, 10c.

No. 26. HOW TO PLAY FOOT BALL

Articles by Walter Camp; Phil King on Quarter Back; L. T. Bliss on Half Back; How to Give Signals and other valuable hints for beginners.

Postpaid, 10c.

No. 27. COLLEGE ATHLETICS

By MICHAEL C. MURPHY, Athletic Director University of Pennsylvania.

Devoted to General Athletics; Latest Method of Training, and a special chapter on Starting.

Postpaid, 10c.

No. 29. PHYSICAL CULTURE

OR EXERCISING WITH PULLEY WEIGHTS.

Arranged by Professor Henry S. Anderson. A Manual of Home Exercise, showing, with correct illustrations, the best exercises for the maintenance of health and the various muscles brought into play.

Postpaid, 10c.

No. 30. LACROSSE

COMPILED BY W. H. CORBETT.

Official Rules of the game, as adopted by the United States Intercollegiate Lacrosse Association.

Postpaid, 10c.

No. 37. ALL AROUND ATHLETICS

By HARRY CORNISH, Director Athletics, Knickerbocker A. C., New York.

Full instructions for the guidance of athletes. Illustrated.

Price, 10c.

No. 32. PRACTICAL BALL PLAYING

By ARTHUR A. IRWIN

Containing interesting chapters on Individual and Team Batting; Essentials of a Good Batsman; Position Bunting; Fielding, etc. With instructive hints to the Pitcher, Catcher, Baseman, Shortstop and Fielders. Fully illustrated.

Postpaid, 10c.

No. 65. Official Book Intercollegiate A. A. A.

Contains the Constitution, By-Laws, List of Clubs and Committees; also the new Athletic Rules and complete record of events since 1876. It gives the tabulated records of points scored by each college since the formation of the Association.

Postpaid, 10c.

No. 71. GOLF MANUAL

A treatise on Golf. History of the Game, Glossary of Technical Terms, Rules of the Game, and other essential points.

Price, 10c.

No. 64. SPALDING'S LAWN TENNIS GUIDE

Edited by J. Parmly Paret. Contains latest rules for playing the game, portraits of prominent players and a record of every important match played during season.

Price, 10c.

No. 68. CROQUET

Revised and corrected by the National Association. Containing latest rules as adopted by the National American Croquet Association.

Price, 10c.

No. 42 PUNCHING BAG

HOW TO USE IT. Full instructions for becoming proficient in this healthful and entertaining exercise.

Price, 10c.

No. 58. BOWLING

Containing instructions How to Bowl, Score, Handicap, and Rules for Playing the various games. Also full records of the prominent bowlers.

Price, 10c.

No. 40. ARCHERY

By JAS. S. MITCHEL

Full Instructions on this Interesting pastime.

Price, 10c.

No. 76. OFFICIAL CYCLE GUIDE

Interesting information for cyclists; portraits of leading riders; complete list of records and other valuable information.

Price, 10c.

No. 77. SPALDING'S ATHLETIC ALMANAC

Compiled by JAMES E. SULLIVAN

Contains all the American and English Amateur Records, complete list of American Champions and Champions of all Associations of the Amateur Athletic Union. It contains portraits of the champions and matter of interest to every athlete in the United States. Only those records are recognized which have been honestly made and are beyond quibble, and our chief aim has been to make this the Official Record Book of Amateur Athletics.

Postpaid, 10c.

No. 69. Official Hand-Book of the A. A. U.

The Constitution, By-Laws, Athletic and General Rules, list of Clubs and Articles of Alliance of the Amateur Athletic Union. The rules have been greatly revised and the changes are plainly indicated by italics. The book is indispensable to every athlete and follower of athletic sports. Illustrated.

Postpaid, 10c.

No. 79. BASE BALL GUIDE FOR 1898

Edited by Henry Chadwick. Contains new rules, full record of all League games and averages for the season; also all minor league statistics, and pictures of all leading Base Ball teams.

Price, 10c.

AMERICAN SPORTS PUBLISHING CO.
16 and 18 PARK PLACE, NEW YORK